SHADES OF EXISTENCE

A CAPTIVATING COLLECTION OF POEMS

MINAKHEE MISHRA

Made with ♥ on the Notion Press Platform
www.notionpress.com

Contents

Contents

Acknowledgements

Sitting on my Grandfather's lap I would fiddle with his huge mole, right at the tip of his nose. "What is this Bapa?" my tiny three-year-old brain asked with genuine ignorance. "Aree you don't know? It's my special power. A nose on my normal nose." Bapa replied with equal authenticity. Pristine in his white dhoti and equally white beard, I used to love spending time in his saintly presence. Today I'm aware of his many special powers, a few being a freedom fighter; his tenure as Editor of Swaraj; being the guru of Princes and Princesses and his grip over language as a medium of communication. Nothing comes from nothing. Certainly, I am what I am thanks to my Grandparents (both maternal & paternal). I will keep the many stories of Bapa, Bou, Aai and Aja for another day. For now, I dedicate this book to my Grandparents and my Parents. A very special thanks to all my family, friends and more who are present with me in my maiden venture through the quotes (both original and borrowed) they sent in. You will find these speckled across the pages of the book as my special mascot, my magic wand. A special thanks to my Mother whose artistic flair has been a big influence in my life. She is the reason I enjoy art and could spin out all the artwork here including the book cover design.

©Minakhee

Foreword

Haraprasad Das (Celebrated Sahitya Akademi & Jnanpith-Moortidevi Award winner Poet & Rtd Civil Service Officer)

"*A first-book wonder, striding triumphantly into the esoteric domain of high poetry, unchallenged by idiomatic modernity.*"

Sruti Mohapatra (Eminent social activist, poet & Nari Shakti Award winner)

"*Minakhee's poems are a journey into our innermost feelings and unexpressed emotions. Her use of vivid imagery and evocative language draws the reader into the core of each poem, provoking reflections on life, feelings and living.*"

1. A Detached Soul

Tread gently on the trail of life
Trample not, waltz nor jive
Egos strewn down the road
One misstep, the façades explode

Feebler than a budding bloom
An old life hanging at its tomb
The slightest fissure or crack
Blood oozes - the pain stark

Bloated balloons tied to money and power
Crammed with uncaring and arid air
Then the string is cut, soul set afloat
Set on an eternal journey on a doomed boat

A detached soul, no strings attached
No fear of raging egos grim
A piece of paper in the harried wind
A buoyant, gleaming, guileless stream

Winning battles with the sword of love

Soothing battered egos in its cradle of simple adore
Accepting all, disowning none
Consuming all
Anger, hatred, criticism, rejection, misconceptions, violence
Consumed by none

Except for truth and love
In its benign core
A detached soul, no strings attached
A piece of paper in the harried wind

Bimala Nanda (Papa)
Listen much, think more, then churn and speak.

2. Kindly Light

You cling on tight
Eyes alone reveal the disquiet
I slept oblivious, you rummaged through worries and plight
"How to shield this tiny life?" you try your might

Avani Chaturvedi, Tessy Thomas, Saina Nehwal or Mary Kom
In your eyes, I'm always the best
For the tiniest step I took, you applauded without rest
For the smallest scratch, I suffered, your heart bruised inside
You hid the fear and drove me to brave the world outside

We may never see things in the same light
You tried to sell me Salwars and long skirts
I craved that shredded jeans and that off-shoulder top
You believed boys can never be friends
For me, except for that special one, most are just friends

You may hunt for my Mr Right
Never stopped me from taking flight
You led me through the jungle called life
Pulled me through when difficult times were rife

Hand in hand through time's weather
You, evolving from maiden to mother
I, blossoming, under your soothing cover
You read my mind when no one could
I blushed; you smiled knowingly and understood

Across life's book, your lessons are knifed
About letting go, even when feelings are rife
Braving the rain to build bridges for other's ease
In the tiniest moments, find life's loveliest breeze
Humanity's truest religion, unconditional love's bliss

Lessons on discovering the common grounds
Embracing the difference without bounds
Forgiving, discarding the hurt and blight
My kindly light, in the darkest night
Word, just writing on the sand- too-cheap brand
Unexplained, uncharted your place in my heartland

<u>Meera (Mom)</u>
All our dreams can come true if we have courage to pursue them.

3. Your Soothing Touch

Save me, God, from this doubt's relentless sway
Lost in indecision's prolonged dismay
Lift me from this pit of unforeseen time
Grant me conviction with your touch divine

Grant me unwavering faith, that night always yields to day's light
After storms waltz, hope persists, a glimmer burning bright
May my faith endure- steadfast, a mountain's reign
Unswayed by fear's whisper, unwavering through disdain

Grant me the armour against scorn's bitter bite
Glimmering gold, forged in trials' fiery plight
In your abode, there are no, commoners or greats
Just the valiant actors, playing their roles, in your set

Ratnaprava (Bou)
Mountains become molehills; A storm becomes a whiff of soothing breeze when you keep your faith in the Almighty.
Uma Prasad (Nana)
Be Good, but never waste your time to prove it. Always remember there is strength within you greater than any storm.

4. Flawless Champion

Pages of time flip on
The book of adore forever young
Which man can compare with your echelon?
Spawns who pale in your comparison

Embellished with patience and kindness
Sheen to your manliness
No crutches of muscles or debonair style
You are still my Tiger in real life

My birth didn't lessen your love for Mom
This girl wasn't disowned, strangled or called a thorn
Treasured -Rocked in your caring hands,
Your dreams for me were grand

You toiled to provide the best
Felt guilty about returning home late
Pained that the sleeping child might forget you
Coz you left home early for that business date

With each step I took

My respect for you grew
Your unpretentious aid for needy crew
Caring for aging parents
When time had stolen, their screw
Always unassuming and modest
My champion- the kindest
It's hard to emulate the sun
Yet I'm determined to trail on
Unchallenged; flawless champion ever born

<u>Alka</u>
Cherish moments; they become memories in a wink.
<u>Zaahirah</u>
Love what you do. Learn every day. Leave a legacy.
<u>Pragnya (Rakhee)</u>
When your destiny and destination are different from others you have to take the road less travelled.

5. My Guide

As I squandered in self-doubt
Heart- aching for some route
You came primed with all your clout
When hope ran its course
Came a silver lining from a divine source
Tugging me from the whirlpool of sand
Trudging me along for that blissful land
"It lies there hidden; don't lose way
Though darkness leads you astray
Unflagging, you must stay"
These glorious words nudged me on
No matter the thousand falls-pricks from the thorns
The hurt from that hurled stone
Uncertainty injecting fears unknown
Rage, insecurity or dread full-blown
It may take ages, but my path is laid
Drenched with bliss glee serenades
Till you are my guide nothing can dissuade

<u>Debjani (Nani)</u>
The quieter you become, the more you are able to hear- Rumi
<u>Lalatendu (Bhaina)</u>
Your relationship is your resilience.

6. Fleeting Serenity

Rustlings through leaves gently,
Serenity strolls stealthily,
Caressing a violet here,
Fondling a rose there.
Smiling at the busy bees,
Relishing the lively butterflies
Soaking in the saccharine melodies
Serenity floats across the morning air

Cuddled in a cradle of bliss,
Oblivious of dangers that glare
Dreams of a sleeping child
And serenity dwells there

The house, in a mess,
Hair tousled and clothes wrinkled
Concocted shrieks of laughter and uproar
Yet serenity defiantly dwells there

Huddled in a lover's embrace
Coming home after a sincere day's work
Breaking the piggy bank for the abandoned boy on that track

Serenity rests clandestinely in these lairs

Often mistaken for its twin, seclusion
Serenity has a nature distinct from its sombre pair

Awaiting an unfaithful lover by the fire,
Drinking silent tears for a son who sleeps in the bier
Aching soul of a child, in a luxury house of Bel Air
Sleepless through the quiet night
Watching for a bomb that might fall anywhere
Oh! Serenity you have cruelly turned your back from there.

Fleeting and short, always in a hurry
Yet such tranquil nectar you ooze in your scurry
You spin your web, charm all, you- deceiving soul
When do you discard your ephemeral role?
Souls lured by your spell,
Lost in your illusory gaze
Devoid of surety or bail
Serenity you are a slippery maze

Debarchan (Bhaina)
Till the full stop does not come, the sentence is not complete.
Jayashree (Bhauja)
Each day life teaches us a new lesson.

©Minakhee

7. Daybreak

A ray of light glitters impatiently, pressing past lush greens
Armed with uncountable promise bursts dawn's first beams

Hope bustles as birds soar on wings of optimism
A new life emerges; the pain of labour elapses
The darkness of night- long obliterated

Gloom pulled out of its shy recesses
There! It stands shamefaced,
gleaming in the rust sparkle of daybreak

The soft chuckle of unbound streams
The soothing touch of silky cool winds
The sunflowers stare boldly, wide-eyed at their beloved king

Always pressed for time, hurry the busy bees
Butterflies flutter adamantly,
labouring to outshine the flowers ceaselessly

Each being bustles, enthused with fresh hope

new energies surge, spilling past horizons
Standing tall, aspiring, attempting
the day is still young

<u>Pinaki</u>
Ability is not how well one plans, but how well he adapts when everything he planned went wrong!
<u>Devendra</u>
Hopeful, positive and full of energy.

8. Birds Of Strong Wings

The day comes to a draw
The squirrels, our neighbours,
squirmed in their tiny craw
Their brood was big, no space to sit still
They are yet to grow

We waited for our parents,
raucous in our little nest
Feathers erect on our body & brow
We hoped for the best
Our stomachs growled, and we moved to and fro

The life of a bird,
not so easy, you see
We court dangers,
just to remain free

Inside that egg,
I felt caged
Bidding my time,
to crack out unfazed

Life has been tough since
We chirped incessantly just to let our parents know
"We are alive; let us grow, just let us grow!"
Eager to leave this nest, eager to go!

A slithering hazard awaits below
Ready to gobble us, that sly fellow
We wish our wings to grow strong
Our will solid to face whatever may go wrong

The nest deceives
Erects a world of make-believe
Danger lurks in the room
Rain, wind and the typhoon loom
The woodcutter at work, the axe is sharp
Ready to strike and attack

Yet life can never be lived in a cocoon
Paradise sans challenges isn't a boon

We wish our wings to grow strong
Our will solid to face anything that may go wrong

<u>Debabrata</u>

A person who does not read has no advantage over one who cannot read. Keep reading.

<u>Divyasa</u>

Striving to be extraordinary while allowing yourself to be happy when you're ordinary.

<u>Devanshu</u>

Embrace every step, whether it's a leap of success or a stumble of failure; in each, find the path to wisdom and growth.

©Minakhee

9. Good Company

Good company is a simple cup of green tea
The promise of fine health & zing minus the inebriation
A climb uphill with heaving breath & soaring spirits
The ache in limbs forgotten, eye ready for joyous sight
A slide down the mountain during the first ski lesson
With each fall comes the glee that I have mastered more
A trail down nature's path enlivened by virgin discoveries
A fluffy squirrel scattering in flight, a flutter of wings delight
A scrumptious book with crispy pages
Engaging, intimate, touching the heart

Debadutta (Mausa)
Action speaks louder than words.
Sudha(Mousi)
You can't change your fate but by changing your habits you can define your destiny.
Arohan
Work is the best form of worship.
Awahan
Books, minds & umbrellas work only when they are open.

©Minakhee

10. Friendship

I discarded the garb of pretence
Unafraid of criticism, sans any defence
Unfazed about rejection
A rare and priceless indulgence
I reveal my true self to you alone
My safety valve during freefall
Never did you leave me forlorn

You fought with kids who teased me
Stirred me on when confidence ceased me
Nudging me along to stand up
Face reality, and step up
We shared invaluable treasures
Silly jokes, secrets, tears: Even fights in good measure

You embraced my vices and virtues unfiltered
My Alchemist, your love- a mountain undeterred

You delighted in my success: Despaired in my failure
Our bond thickened neither by blood nor by relation
Cemented neither by constraint nor by conformity

Strengthened neither by obligation nor by duty
A thread of unconditional adore binds
Unseen, untarnished and unbroken
Tied ceaselessly through all dimension

<u>Leon & Lorraine</u>
Life is living the virtue of LOVE over everything.
<u>Upasana</u>
Smile and let everyone know that today you are a lot stronger than you were yesterday.
<u>Swapna</u>
In our endeavour to become a better version developing universal empathy should remain our highest goal.

11. Gift Hunting

A soft shawl drenched in love; a few dainty home décor
A smile across Mom's face, that's for sure
A smart shirt; savvy gadgets for the car
Now my bro is loading me with presents without par
Branded purses, perfumes and souvenirs
Gifts for the rest, I manage without an uproar

Father, I heard you wore the sweater till it tore
Mom secretly discarded it before it became family joke lore
Never demanding, considerate and loving
Treasuring gifts for their intrinsic worth

Gift hunting for loved ones? Nah! It's not a chore
For dads? An arduous mission to the core
Shirts, pens and sweaters- their cabinets overflow
Some novelty? You know what's in store
"I don't need anything." Those words spring for sure
Blink! The gifts vanish behind closed cupboard doors

Any promotion or award I got
Bro's success at the race and life in a good spot
Dad's pleasure is unmatched

Yet this time I'm taking a branded watch.

<u>Dr. Narayan (Uncle)</u>

He who serves best profits most.

<u>Asha (Aunty)</u>

Grab your dream before it's too late.

<u>Anindita</u>

Perspective is everything in life. One man's shack is another man's palace.

<u>Puspita</u>

Failure germinates the future.

12. Cradle Of Happiness

Happiness, stealthily taking tender strides
you tiptoed into my barren land.
Never did I reckon your soft
steps on the sand.

Opening the doors of my shabby life,
you lead me to the joyous light.
Shaded from the blight by your
benevolent sight.

A tiny dream housed in
my gullible heart,
I chased after butterflies, deluding my gasp.
The warmth of a mother's embrace,
a sweet goodnight kiss,
a father's encouraging pat, was it too much to ask?

Grains of hope escaped my tiny fingers,
seeking to seize a drop of bliss.
The childhood joys, the unwritten rights of all naïve hearts,
always gave me a miss.

A lonely bird forsaken by its kind.
A speck of dust deserted-
to face the perils of life.
No place to rest; there was none to call my
own.

Yet happiness caught me unaware-
Alighting tenderly like birds on a branch.
Startled, captivated by its soothing arrival,
I fell silently into its gentle lap.
Lulled to a restful sleep,
after a long, weary walk.

You picked me up from the garbage bin.
Called me your precious life,
not a sin.
Hushed me to sleep in a cozy bed.
Now I have a home,
it's no longer a dream.

Goodnight kisses, a protective hug,
no longer an illusion struggling to thrive.
I dare to touch the sky.
Let innocence run wild in the cradle of life.
No, grieve or pain can come to pry,

for I have the will to be alive.

<u>Divya</u>

Parenting: The most important job in the world requires no certification or licence.

©Minakhee

13. The Light Of Life

The radiance of night plays tricks on the mind
Is it day yet? Oh! it's just the luminous Diwali lights
Fountains of laughter ignite the air
Spirited children and sparkles sprinkle happiness blare
Shiny glitters wipe away the gloomy shades
Everywhere life and the zeal to live thrives

Elsewhere, the air shatters, and splinters fly
Screeches of terror vibrate through every inch
A line of houses reduces to boulders and ashes dry
Panic, fear, and shrieks of desperation descend
A hand, a leg, bloody faces dots every inch
Innocence, humanity and sanity mutilated; only brutality rages thick

For land, honor, religion or money, the reason forever weak
The right to erase life can never be a worthy feat

Rajan
In hindsight, every decision is suboptimal. Be fearless in your choices, and continue to march forward.

©Minakhee

14. Tale Of A River

Once my fronts swelled with pride
Vibrant weeds and innocent child
Unafraid of the tide,
danced with abandon by my side.

Once, my blue expanses glittered like gold
Bathed in formidable sun's rays, bold
Once, when the soothing moon smiled
I gleamed like a diamond, exquisite and wild

Hoards of plastic now choke my bed
Repulsive stench swells from faeces laid
Bloated corpses of lively creatures
That once added jest to my features
Float upstream, suffocating my very being

Stripped of dignity and deprived
Helpless now, at your mercy as you thrive
Yet, if I am dead: Every bit of life sucked from my bed
Haunted by the ghosts of your deed, you, too, will bleed

<u>Lopamudra</u>

Be the reason someone believes in the goodness of people.

<u>Sandeep</u>

Knowledge speaks but wisdom listens. Purpose fuels passion. Storms make trees that take deeper roots.

©Minakhee

15. Greatest Teacher

Life- the greatest teacher, it's said
Often in unfathomable dialect, it is laid
Casing a concealed message unread
Apparent at some distant time: The meaning now fade

Life –the untiring coach
Casts a tender glance sometimes on approach
The sweet cradle of a mother, humming a soft rhyme
Beware! The foliage transforms in no time
Warm colors of Spring turn savage
Angry Summer then rages
The road ahead runs into a dead-end
The kayak of happiness tossed at the next bend

Lessons are taught through annals of times-
"Control your desire, master your will"
"Then the world will be at your feet - deal!"
Yet desire always betrays
A wild child un-reined, running astray!
Will- easily trapped becomes desire's prey!

Battles are waged for freedom still

Revolting for the Right to Free Will
Sacrifices have to be made- that's the drill
Innocent blood will have to be spilled

Liberty then dons the white gown
Independence arrives- an angel with a crown
Alas! Democracy is caged again
Coz demons within rise- that's the bane
Will succumbs to free will
Greed and corruption conquer still
Do good and get the same return?
Nah!
Alas! The good always burn

Life's lesson changes into another set
Do Good and Just Forget!
Surly you get your return in another birth
Evil will burn in hell, if not on earth

It's strange these lessons of life- such fallacies
Defective with expired warranties
Bereft of interest and guarantees
No rules in God's banana republics

The young and healthy dies

Goodness suffers, and evil flies
The message of life is still unclear, unread
Surely in a foreign dialect, it's laid

<u>Amol</u>
Never be so busy as to not think of others.
<u>Bhairavi</u>
There is nothing either good or bad, but thinking makes it so.

©Minakhee

16. Courageous Grey World

In the courageous world of grey
She treads with grace, night and day
Within her frail form, a fire resides
No barrier shakes the faith inside
"I'm free, I'm strong," her quiet refrain

Etched lines tell tales of endless care
Sacrifice echoes in each crease there
Her forehead, a map of countless pains
Of worry for kin, of maternal strain
The hidden flames ablaze, yet veiled

Time whispers to her softly, urging rest's embrace
Revel in the glory, slow your pace
But fumbles and falls mark her stride
She shuns help and pushes support aside
Her turmoil is hidden behind her quiet Might

Past and present become entangled yarns
Her mind a maze of endless knotted turns
Scattered visions demand her sight

Smiles of dead brother unseen by light
A world where time's boundaries blur and bite

Youth calls her senile, old in their gaze
Oblivious of the strength within that maze
In her mirage world, courage resides
Walking between two realities in her ageing mind
Driven by her soul's fortitude she is a miracle maligned

<u>Soni</u>
Take what you learnt and become a better person.
<u>Sulagna</u>
You've shown remarkable courage by taking bold risks & achieving meaningful milestones in your life.

17. Godless Land

Glorious morning, gleaming light
Chirping birds, sweet fragrance glides
The heart takes flight, soars with might
God's creations, truly bright

Dying eyes, blackened faces, tangled hair
Tiny bodies in tatters or bare
Stifled childhood, swanky limbs
Groping smelly dustbins and broken dreams

Glorious morning, gleaming light
Are God's creations truly bright?
Strings of doubt clutch tight
God must have turned deaf and dim of sight

The mystery deepens and unravels at times
Questions and answers delicately twined
Each left to drown or stay alight
In torrid mornings, burning light

<u>Dr. Vasudev (Mamu)</u>

If we judge people no nobody is ours. If we understand people everyone is ours.

<u>Ramakrishna (Mamu)</u>

When you get what you want, that is God's direction. When you don't get what you want, that is God's protection.

©Minakhee

18. Trials On The Trail Of Life

What is this furore?
Why this uproar?
No murderer or sinner
I'm no criminal or offender

I walk, I run
Exploring new terrain
With the jest of a child
Just learning to toddle and stride

I fear not a fall,
nor getting bruised or burnt
Learning each day,
with faith in my heart

I may fumble or trip
Bleed from stones and slip
Lose my way a bit on a dark alleyway
But you have sanctified my path, I can't stray

But with my resolve is strong, my destination untainted.
You, Master Maker, will smooth out my wounds.
At the end of the dark tunnel, there will be your glowing light-
Illuminating my being, erasing the pain,
for I would have passed each test and each trial on life's lane.

<u>Deepshika</u>
Life is a game. You become a champion by fighting one more round!
<u>Malvika</u>
The beauty of any first time is that it leads to a thousand others - Pico Iyer

19. Heaven & Hell Here & Now

Why am I still stuck in this mire?
Why isn't there light in this tunnel dire?
Lead oh! kindly light, I deserve it
It has been ages since I asked for my bit

With grit and passion, I tilled the soil
Hope spread generously, clipping wings to my toil
Seeds of faith adorned my destined land
Sweats of hard work to irrigate, they joined hands

Yet, at birth, the sapling was nipped
Now its withered remains dripped
Actions speak louder than words, I had heard
"Labor! Sweet fruits will follow", I had heard
Yet you were deaf to my prayers
Forget fruits sweet, I was broken at each layer

Defying the storms, this reed stood still
Yet, your boon showered at another's bid?

No rivalry propels me for your tender grace
Nor chasing ambition, I come to your place
Yet, torn to find no glance at my path
Am I not your child? Why this divergence from divine math?
Why are scales tilted in favor of some?
Why abandon me in the sinking boat alone?

Have I sinned- Or even spoken a harsh word?
Have I hurt someone deep and hard?
I question and tussle with the past
Looking for meaning to your behavior harsh

Oh, divine guide, grant this plea I raise
Let my paradise, my inferno, in this life blaze
For deeds, both good and those that mar
No ledger beyond, no karmic bar
In human frailty, my memories faint
I will no longer query your math, divine saint

Let the soil glitter with sincere toil
Let the harvest bloom with faith and hope unsoiled,
Let there be no suspect or inquiry of why, when and how
Let my heaven and hell be here and now

<u>Biswajit</u>

Be not afraid of growing slowly be afraid of standing still.

<u>Jaya</u>

Happiness lies in acceptance.

20. Justice Drugged

Long after her cries died, a scream crippled her being still
She kept pushing that invisible hand muffling her voice still
The tears had dried, yet her soul wept
The silence disturbing like eerie spiders crept

Justice stared muted, blinded and drugged

When demons scarred, slapped, bite, and ravaged her
Laughing at her ordeal, giddy in their savage spur
The thought thumping in her mind,
"If I live through this hell, I'll have your death bond signed"

Justice lay still as if on its deathbed

The nation was enraged in her grief
A cause to stir their souls stiff
Skins thickened, now melted, in her burning pain
Their sensitivity awakened against the sickening bane

Justice woke from comma but slipped again

Memories fade, interest wanes, her bloodied scars healed
Yet her fiery dignity's screams can never be sealed
She has been stripped a thousand times in court
"All for Justice " they still dote

Justice now mocks in its drugged spur

For Justice, she has to pay a toll
Battle the raging war within to repair her battered soul
The Promised Land still remains a distant dream
A puppet of Justice's incessant, innumerable whims

Yes, Justice has been drugged, and her fate is sealed

Sweta
There is nothing called a "Problem", it's the absence of an idea to find the solution.
Sumeeta
Self-love is the highest form of love.

©Minakhee

21. Carnage And Creation

The carnage has ceased
The wind? Long since fallen limp
The fiery storm, no longer orchestrating a rampage
It has abandoned its mission grim

Tearing here, twisting there, brutally raging a scuffle everywhere
The ruins are scattered- belongings in a careless teenager's room
The scars were deep, raw and bleeding
Every wound open, howling over the doom

I sit there amidst the debris like a barmy in tatters
The beautiful edifice collapsed in batters
The remains lay scattered, screaming, screeching, twisting in anguish
This is all that is left: a handful of sand from the castle- I languish

The past is gone and lost in time
No ramblings in ifs, whys, and buts of life,
can ever bring it back alive
So, I cling to the relics like a mother cuddling her sick child in the dark

Never has there been a more urgent dread
These remnants are mine to call,
they never left my side
What if even these fade?

Only these scraps were mine,
the rest is just an illusion of a wandering mind
There aren't any roofs to keep out the rain,
but the sun still shines bright and not in disdain

I still can brave another day
Build a structure on these snippets grey
A modest edifice, airy and clean,
with room enough for all my dreams

<u>Shivani</u>
Continuously endeavoring to enhance oneself daily, thereby evolving into an elevated and refined iteration of personal excellence.

©Minakhee

22. Life & Death

Vibrant flowers, chirping birds,
Soothing winds, a cool bed of green grass
Rainbows in the sky, laughing children dash
Soft touch of a lover, the chuckle of a little lass
Life, I thought, was about that

A raging storm inside her heart,
Eyes were of stone, darts shredding her apart
The living corpse called Mom, grieving her precious part
Her mouth stitched, nursing her lads ailing dad
Life, I hear, is a sonnet so sad

Her soul ripped: Innocence battered
Struggling to piece together her honor, tattered
A scream zipped to her lips
The demons haunt her dreams
Life, I see, has infinite knives unseen

Death, all say, is the opposite of life
Soothing winds, a cool bed of green grass
Rainbows in the sky, laughing children dash
The soft touch of a lover, the chuckle of a little lass

Death must be, is like that

<u>Syeda</u>

Time doesn't heal emotional pain, you need to learn how to let go.

23. Free In Love

The shackles are broken
Each cell is jubilant: It's free
No longer bonded to false promises
never falling into that spree

Words and assurances of love
Letters written on sand
A whiff of wind,
it all goes bland

When the hurricane blazed,
who held the roof despite blistered hands?
When the flames threatened to consume,
who braved the fire, jumping from the stands?
Wasted not a moment in baseless phrases,
sang endless love ballads with actions un-tired

True love? It ain't defined by needs & wants
Liberated from obligations and self-made prisons
Two soul mates, sky and sea, meeting on the horizon
Separate identities, yet co-existing till eternity
Freed from expectations and demands

Inseparable and yet separate they stand

<u>Karteekka</u>

Finding love within yourself completes the beautiful story of who you are.

24. The Wait

The wait has been long
The night, thousand shades dark and stark
Patience plays hide-and-seek
Hope balances only on the strings of past

When faith ran its course,
mistrust gobbled the pages of unspoken trust
Strings were severed,
the crippled limb slashed

Alas! Oh, heart always a fool,
easily duped, gropes for some pleasant route
So the faded light flickers again,
chopped limbs grow back: The concealed ache bounces back

Memories creep and crawl, beckoning, sprinkling balm
Soothing the hurt, projecting those beautiful times
Inciting to hold the post, churning out the dirt
I rummage, for sane reason, for the unprovoked backlash

Optimism clings to fragile strings

Perhaps you will visit my lane
Hold my hands, smile at me,
Even share a cup of tea

Brief me through the pages of years gone by:
The time your brows turned wrinkled from shiny
Will you still listen with equal zest
Share a laughter here, a tear there without any fear

Your Memories stand lonely
Alive and Real
Your actual existence?
Why hasn't it ever come near?

No plea, penance or remorse in sight
No recompense or acts to right the wrongs
A plain farewell before my final flight
Grant me a moment; it has been long

Waiting to say you are long forgiven
That anger long forgotten
Love has triumphed,
friendship strong and still in charge

<u>Swapnasri</u>

Let yourself become a living poetry.

<u>Sthitiprangya</u>

Life is too short to worry or be sorry, pick your mojo and go make merry!

©Minakhee

25. Unpredictable Love

Your love, my sweet, the lashing sting of unseasonal rain
An unpredictable child
A vast, enigmatic ocean
I try to keep afloat in vain
I took the plunge, flapping far from the nest of love
Faith clouding my judgment
Belief tricking and shoving
Thrilled into Cupid's unknown land, I drove

The fury fermenting within you?
Must be your possessive love
I blushed within your protective cage
Must be your untamed adore
The dust of time settled on our nuptial ties
Delusional blindfolds are gone, revealing the rotting lies

I walked through fire to please you
Changed my attire- my thoughts- down to my very soul
Yet, with every alteration comes a sterner demand
Striking to fracture my very core

Your triumphs, my joy; Your defeats, my sorrow
I'm always your unswerving companion- Don't we belong?
Yet your hand fails me when the blizzards blow strong
In sickness, while I nurse you, your cruel snides, I ignore
"Perhaps it's your pain talking," I think no more
Yet wounds unseen take their toll- like a growing bedsore

When my heart cries out, I nurse my broken dreams alone
You think of me as clingy- deserving to be left forlorn
What if I let the truth stand stripped
Bared of impulse, mirage and fantasy- not tightlipped
Pristine in the light of realization- It says, yes, love seeks no reward
But has a bleak fate unadorned by mutual admiration and regard

<u>Sunita (Nani)</u>
It's always nice to talk to my bubbly little sister.

26. Illegitimate Widow

Wandering across the heartless night,
ashes of unfulfilled desires glide
Fanning the blaze, broken promises rage,
stepping on troubled water- taking center stage

There I spot you, offender, love barterer, trust slaughterer
You lay rested in your auburn casket lair
Sporting a smirk that taunts me, even in your bier
"I have eluded you", you snide without so much as a word
Even fate has stamped on your devious pact; what a charade!

Your appearance familiar,
expression unknown to my sight
No sign of tempestuous vigor,
possessing you in those hushed stolen nights
Your pristine widow,
keeper of your chaste image
Your innocuous children,
untouched by the betrayal still, dwell in a mirage
Broken only by grief, unsullied in your death
A heavy debt rests solely on my every breath

None discern the fire destroying my very being
The twin, burden of love and treachery casting a deadly ring
The new life spurting within,
your momentary love or lust playing on our mind
Is it our love child or the blunder of the blind?
A victim of your charm, idol worshiper, your slave
My follies snigger at me,
an open wound decaying, to be carried to my grave

<u>Sambit</u>

A day should begin with optimism and end with gratitude

27. Cruel Love

The day comes to a draw
Shamefaced, the sun hides
The south winds blow
Memories come in full flow

Those careless accusations fly
Each time they hit the bull's eye
Each time they stung
Pierced at some deeper rung

Then, the mind resolved to stay strong
An adamant face, a counter-attack flung
Inside, the heart never ceased to cry
Love makes one weak-willed
Clinging onto a lover like an addictive pill

Happiness- never be enslaved to another's will
Happiness - always be bound to internal purpose and zeal
Is it hard to comprehend for a rational mind?
Alas, love robs sanity
Caging it in a mindless grind!

<u>Smita</u>

When this heart melts, feelings are unshackled, the inner being flows as poetry. Coming from there it's all about his expression.

<u>Pinky</u>

Life is as beautiful as you can make it.

©Minakhee

28. The White Widow

• 63 •

In the hushed, muted nights, a stifled cry spills
Across the lonely fields, the lone willow still

My throat parched and dried my eyes now of stone
Even tears have deserted me only your sweet memories gnaw

There on that bed, we talked through the night
Drowned in love and tenderness, sleep lost its might

Out on the lawn, we drenched in the rain
Laughter and absurd joy ran through our vein

There in that cupboard hangs your stiff shirt
Loyal companion currently, humoring my insane chat

Thrown on the chair, your unkempt towel sits
The scent of your being lingers in every bit

Raiding through the moments of warmth,

silly fights, my lover, my friend
Your memories are my crutches till the end

<u>Ivan</u>
The only way to discover the limits of the possible is to go beyond them into the impossible.
<u>Nandan</u>
Don't let Yesterday take too much of today!

29. Sweetheart

Her heart was now deadened- barren.
Instincts a crippled terrain.
For the rosy bundle on her lap,
no love spurred; Just a gnawing gap.

"Look, it's a girl!" The nurse smiled.
She glanced at the squirming child.
It stunned her! What's this?
The creature had a halo of bliss!

"This is the devil's child"
Every inch of her mind cried.

The bile of bitterness erupted.
Her ears burnt crimson and heated.
A thousand needles pricked.
As insane hatred brimmed.

A shriek escaped her mouth "Aaah!
Startled, the little one wailed!
Now the tot resembled a tiny her.

Something in her turned.
It caught her unaware- she burned.

Her pain resurfaced! The agony rushed back.
The scars threatened to bleed and crack.

Trapped in the monster's lair-
she felt the beast rip her soul apart.
The onslaught on her body stack.
That body she once claimed as her own-
Brutalized, tarnished, torn, ransacked.

The baby wailed.
She snapped back.

"Is this cherub in pain too?"
She was recalled from the dark.

Within her, seasons changed.
Everything became a muddle.
Blood rushed to her thirsty heart.
She clung to the bawling bundle.
The mother in her crumbled.

She knew she had to fight back.
Rest the skeletons in her past.

Beat the shame and mockery;
make it a haven for her sweetheart.

<u>Ritu</u>
When you evoke the desire of be better, each day is an opportunity for growth, kindness, and self-improvement.
<u>Dr. Leena</u>
Life with its incessant crests and troughs is a great teacher

30. Love: Bliss Or Misery

An echo reverberates
The thumping in my heart is strong
Breaching the safe walls of solitude
All that I feared, now I long

That soft touch
The half-lit smile
The lashes simmering on almond eyes
Yes, I once dwelled in that paradise

Seasons took a wink to change
Spring turned to bitter winter, deranged

Once I had escaped the cages of love
Deep cuts and bruises I concealed for a long
Solitude I befriended and never left its side
Now, love seeps in slyly past my pride

My mind plays tricks,
I feel ready to forsake my claim to the sky
The past looks hazy

I crave captivity -ready to pay the prize

Caught at crossroads
swaying between bliss and misery
Walking through paradise
or courting a forgotten injury

Rashmi (Aunty)
Be faithful to that which exists within you!
Anand Raj Ok
Outside of a dog, a good book is a man's best friend. Inside of a dog, it's too dark to read.- with apologies to Groucho Marx.

About The Author

Minakhee Mishra is a storyteller at heart who feels life's too short for bland tales and ice-creamless diets. Deep into the corporate world as an Editor and Brand Marketer, she finally listened to her inner voice to release restless creative energy within. As they say, it is never too late.

In a constant quest for inner engineering, she feels degrees and professional achievements don't define a person. With a professional job as an Editor and Brand Marketer, she is entangled in her day-to-day affairs in the realms of B2B and SaaS industries. Minakhee's academic journey includes multiple post-graduations: one in Sociology, one in Advertising and market Research and one in Marketing Management. These provide her with a strong foundation for understanding human behaviour and effectively crafting compelling narratives.

Diving into the vast ocean of contemporary topics, Minakhee has authored numerous articles that have garnered recognition in multiple publications. Her contributions have earned her the prestigious title of First Brand Ambassador of Times of India in the NRI section. You will also find her inked adventures in Khaleej Times, Gulf News, Art mags, etc. With a diverse range of interests, she fearlessly delves into discussions about Art, Lifestyle, SaaS and Technology, enriching her readers' lives with her insights.

Beyond her professional achievements, she loves taking frequent detours to visit her passion for writing, art and travel. She is an avid blogger, sharing her creative endeavours on her website, Buzzingtales (https://www.buzzingtales.com) - her creative cocoon— which buzzes with musings on art, writing, and her globetrotting escapades. Through this digital window, she invites readers into the vivid tapestry of her escapades in the realms of writing and art.